# More guitar Workshop

## by Jim Kelly

Berklee Press is the official publishing division of the Berklee College of Music, the premier institution for the study of music today. Berklee Press produces practical books, video tapes, DVDs, and interactive products for musicians, students, teachers, and hobbyists. Our products focus on all areas of contemporary music education including performance, ear training, harmony, composition, songwriting, arranging, film scoring, music therapy, production, engineering, music business, synthesis, and music technology.

Berklee Press
1140 Boylston Street
Boston, MA 02215, USA Tel: 617-747-2146

ISBN 0-7935-9454-5

**Berklee**
PRESS

DISTRIBUTED BY

7777 W. BLUEMOUND RD. P.O. BOX 13819 MILWAUKEE, WI 53213

# Contents

# Thanks

I would like to thank all my family: my parents, Jim and Anne, for helping every step of the way, including buying that first electric guitar; my wife Meg who gave the love, support, and room to develop this music; and my kids, Matt and Kate, for being the great people they are.

Thanks to the guys in the band—Jim Odgren, Bob Tamagni, Bob Killoran, and Christian Bausch—for bringing the charts to life.

There are so many people at the college I should thank, but I must mention Larry Baione, Rick Peckham, Tony Marvuglio, Matt Marvuglio, Larry Monroe, and Tom Riley, who have helped greatly in getting this material out. Also thanks to Fender Musical Instruments for their help.

Lastly, I must thank all the students and friends who have helped by working through this material at the college and abroad: I hope you recognize some of it.

Jim

# Credits

**Audio**
Jim Kelly: Guitar
Bob Tamagni: Drums
Jim Odgren: Alto Sax
Bob Killoran: Electric Bass
Christian Fabian Bausch: Acoustic Bass
Rob Jaczko: Producer/Engineer
Tony Marvuglio: Associate Producer
Mike Barrett, Alex Chan, and Tracy Vail:
Assistant Engineers

**Project Manager**
Debbie Cavalier

**Cover Design**
Dave Miranda

**Layout**
Dave Miranda

**Copyediting**
Lisa Burrel
Jonathan Feist

**Text Transcription**
Steve Melisi

**Special thanks to:**
President Lee Eliot Berk
Gary Burton
Dave Kusek

**Additional thanks to:**
David Mash
Bill Scheniman
Sherry Baker
Mark Wolinski
Joe Hostetter
Rob Hayes
Rob Rose
Dorothy Messenger
Kim Grant
Eric Hanselman

# Audio CD

| Track # | Title | Specifics | Timing |
|---|---|---|---|
| 1 | A LITTLE WES | | 4:32 |
| 2 | STILL PRETENDIN' (distorted solo) | | 3:26 |
| 3 | STILL PRETENDIN' (clean solo) | | 3:26 |
| 4 | BOUNCIN' WITH RICK | | 2:50 |
| 5 | STUDY IN G MINOR (Two Down, One Up) | | 1:48 |
| 6 | FELLINI | | 1:07 |
| 7 | METERMAN | | 5:16 |
| 8 | MUTT & JEFF | | 6:26 |
| 9 | TUNING NOTES | | :22 |
| 10 | USED BLUES | | :55 |
| 11 | USED BLUES | Play-along | :55 |
| 12 | SONG FOR AN IMAGINARY VOCAL (Acoustic Style) | | 4:30 |
| 13 | SONG FOR AN IMAGINARY VOCAL (Acoustic Style) | Play-along | 4:28 |
| 14 | LATIN-STYLE BLUES (pick) | | 1:14 |
| 15 | LATIN-STYLE BLUES (fingers) | | 1:16 |
| 16 | A LITTLE WES | Play-along | 4:32 |
| 17 | STILL PRETENDIN' | Play-along | 3:26 |
| 18 | BOUNCIN' WITH RICK | Play-along | 2:48 |
| 19 | METERMAN | Play-along | 5:16 |
| 20 | MUTT & JEFF | Play-along | 6:20 |

# Introduction

Hello and welcome to "More Guitar Workshop". First off let me say that if you have never seen volume 1 of this series, don't worry; they are not designed to be sequential. As with the former book, the music and studies in this collection are for a variety of levels.

If you are studying on your own, I suggest listening to the recording and following along with the music. Depending on your experiences you can choose where to begin and which stuff to put off until a later date. If you are a teacher, you can look over the music and choose the pages that will best relate to, help, and hopefully inspire your students.

Some of this music was intended as studies, but quite a bit of it I use as songs to play in concerts and clubs. Much of the material works well in a band situation without an excessive amount of rehearsal. I think the strongest part of this material is that it's usable for a group. Don't worry if you don't have players at the present time because the guitar tracks are removed on the second half of the CD to make it a play-along. The intent of the recording was to make as "live" a feel as possible.

So good luck with the book. I hope it helps in your pursuit of learning and enjoying guitar and music.

Jim Kelly

# A LITTLE WES

**Audio CD Tracks**
Band            1
Play-along    16 (no guitar solo)

Intro: 8 bars

In Head: twice

Written Solo: 1 chorus

Guitar Solo: 3 choruses

Out Head: once

This is a dedication to Wes Montgomery—without question, one of the greatest jazz guitarists the world will ever know. The feel and the harmony of this tune are similar to some of the things he wrote and played. It's a 16-bar form that's basically in the key of G minor. In fact, you can get through most of the piece by ear, staying in the G minor blues sound.

One of the more difficult aspects of this piece is knowing how and when to take advantage of arpeggios and scales not directly in the key. This is one thing that Wes could do incredibly well. For example, in the 4th bar of the tune, when the G minor shifts to the G7 sound. He could set up the resolution into the Cm7 from the G7 with some hip-sounding scale or arpeggio line. The blues sound would still work here, but a little research gives more options that can lend these sorts of jazz connections to your solos.

A real drawback to playing only by ear is that you can miss a lot of stuff if you're just guessing what chord scales or notes will fit. Take the 6th bar, for example, where the chords are Bbm7 to Fb9. The blues scale isn't the best choice because some notes just don't fit. This section can seem treacherous and foreign. Try playing around the notes in the chord (the chord tones). Since both chords are related to Bb Dorian (Ab major scale), listen to how these other notes sound when added to the chord tones.

It takes a long time to understand and feel comfortable with chords that are shifting keys. Many tunes are like this: you can group most chords into the same key, but there are places where the chords are from another key (non-diatonic). By studying these places, you can improve the way your lines connect.

On the recording, we played an 8-bar intro vamp. Often these kinds of intros are open (not set in length), although the phrases would typically be 4 bars long. The melody is played twice at the beginning, then I played a one-chorus written solo that is intended to sound like ideas Wes might have played. This solo is all around the lower positions and in a register that Wes favored. To go for that Wes-like tone, I used my thumb instead of a pick.

I don't think anyone else will ever be as fluent with this style as he was, but it's a great sound and lends itself to experimenting. Try slides and such since "thumbing" each note doesn't work as well with this approach.

After the solos, the melody can be played once or twice. The ending is a vamp on the intro chord changes. When playing live, try to fade out the ending.

# A Little Wes

Jim Kelly

Medium Swing (♩ = 132)

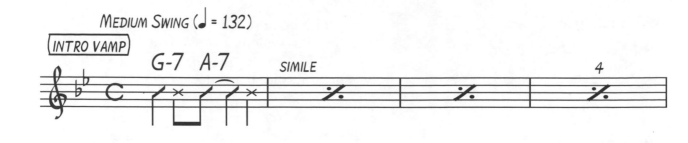

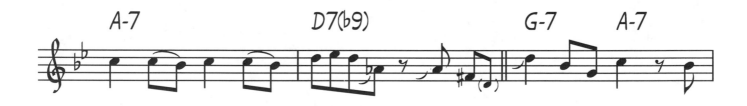

WRITTEN SOLO CHORUS

CONTINUE SOLOING

# STILL PRETENDIN'

**Audio CD Tracks**

| | |
|---|---|
| Band | 2 (distorted solo) |
| | 3 (clean solo) |
| Play-along | 17 (no lead guitar) |

Intro: 8 bars

In Head: 1 chorus

Guitar Solo: 3 choruses

This one is an acoustic style groove that lends itself to a pentatonic-type solo approach. It is a 16-bar tune based in 3 keys. The 8-bar intro is the I chord to the IV chord in the key of E over an E bass (an E pedal). These chords also make up the second half of the form: the second eight. The first 6 bars of the form consist of the IV chord to the I chord in the key of A. Bars 7 and 8 are IV to I in the key of G.

You will notice that, with the exception of the E major triad, all the other chords are labeled "add9." This chord sound consists of the 1, 3, 5, and 9 from the major scale and contains no 7th.

Cadd9 has the notes C, E, G, and D. The 9 is the same pitch as the 2nd of the scale. The order of the notes is often changed: for example 1, 5, 9, and 3. This chord sound is used in contemporary music of all styles and often in this acoustic-style rhythm playing.

Since the add9 has no 7th in the voicing, it can be used as a substitute for chords that contain a major 7th or dominant 7th. Another way of using it is to add interest to a triad voicing. For instance, substituting Aadd9 for A.

A related chord symbol you will see for Cadd9 is C2, sometimes labeled Csus2. C2 consists of the notes C, D, and G: the 1, 2, and 5 of the chord. Often the 1 or the 5 is doubled in the voicing. Since there is no 3rd in the voicing, this sound can be used as a "sub" (substitute) for major and minor: for example, the progression E2 to C2 can sub for Em to C.

Getting back to the song, the voicings are at the bottom of this page. Listen to the recording for the rhythmic feel and try some variations of your own. It's constant 16th-note strumming, and you can practice it on acoustic and electric guitar. The melody is simple. Try adding other slides or bends when you like. The trickiest part is soloing because the key changes take a while to connect. Think melody and, since it has a sort of folk feel, try lines that fit in that groove.

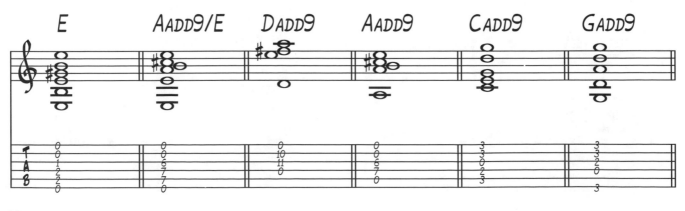

# STILL PRETENDIN'

Jim Kelly

Acoustic 16th Feel (♩ = 88)

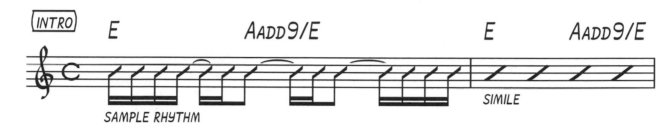

# BOUNCIN' WITH RICK

**Audio CD Tracks**

Band            4

Play-along      18 (no lead guitar)

Intro: 2 bars

In Head: once

Guitar Solo: 3 choruses

Out Head: once with tag

This song was written to play at a concert with a faculty group of four guitars, bass, and drums and is fittingly called "Guitar Frenzy." Rick Peckham is the assistant chair of the Guitar Department at Berklee and the organizer of that concert. He knows that I write a lot, and he requested that I contribute some tunes. This is one of the tunes that I decided to contribute. The head is part Charlie Parker, part John Scofield, and right up Rick's alley.

The form is 32-bar *AABA:* standard in jazz. Each section is 8 bars long, and all the *A* sections are exactly the same chords and melody. The melody is harder during the *A* section than on the bridge: see pages 40 and 41 for fingering suggestions.

The whole tune consists of dominant 7th chords, much like the blues. Since the bridge doesn't sound that different than the *A* section, it's easy to get lost in the form. Try to count and feel for when the top comes around. One thing to listen for is the bridge: it's the only 8-bar section that doesn't begin on the I chord: the F7. The *B* section (or "bridge") starts on the IV chord: the Bb7. This marks the halfway point of the form.

Soloing over the "form" (the chord progression of a tune) is one of the key skills of a jazz player. This style of soloing is rare in rock and happens in blues, but mostly over the 12-bar form. Jazz tunes have many different lengths. Whenever you listen to a jazz recording, try to follow the form. This is kind of an obvious statement, but it's easily overlooked.

Dominant 7th chords offer the most choices in terms of scales to play, and choosing from those scales is a continuous process of studying and experimenting.

On the recording, I tried to stay close to the chord sounds and blues lines with some added chromatic notes, nothing very "out." Rick plays some really interesting and strange stuff on this type of progression; ask him what it is if you see him.

# BOUNCIN' WITH RICK

Jim Kelly

Medium Up Swing (♩ = 126)

Tag last two bars for ending

(blank page to facilitate page turn)

# STUDY IN G MINOR
## (TWO DOWN, ONE UP)

**Audio CD Track**
Solo Guitar  5

This is a classical-style solo guitar study. The idea was to write an exercise for getting comfortable playing wide intervals with a pick. If you look at the music, you'll see that the notes are spaced quite far apart. Much of the piece is based on spread or "open" triads. Instead of arpeggiating in a closed position, you displace the middle note by an octave. For example, a G minor triad is spelled G, B♭, D (1, ♭3, 5). An open version could be G, D, B♭ (1, 5, ♭3). This is the first arpeggio of the piece.

Another related sound is the same open sound applied to 7th chords. The arpeggios in this study are all three notes, and since a 7th chord has four notes you have to leave one out. The notes of D7, for instance, are D, F♯, A, and C. The next arpeggio in the first measure contains three of these four notes: the F♯ is not used. Music written for violin and cello often utilizes these open sounds partly, I believe, because these instruments are tuned in fifths and open voicings are more natural to this tuning.

On the guitar, these wide intervals require some string skipping that is awkward with a pick. The easiest way I found to play it is using two down strokes followed by one up stroke, (the study's subtitle). I use this picking throughout the piece. Feel free to try other ways of playing. One way is to pick it with your fingers. This makes a lot of sense if you are playing a nylon string guitar. Another possibility would be to play the down strokes with the pick and the up stroke with your middle finger: a pick and finger combination. This is also a good way to play wide intervals on the guitar. Bill Frisell and Eric Johnson come to mind as players who use this approach.

Try to analyze the three-note grouping as best you can. See if you can figure out what chords are implied. I suggest doing this with any classical-style piece you try to learn. It will help you visualize and understand how the chords are put together.

Once you have figured out the notes, practice at a slow tempo with a metronome. I think it feels best when played a little rubato: that is, slowing down a little during certain phrases. Listen to the recording for ideas.

Remember, it's an exercise, but try to play it as musically and accurately as you can. I still find it challenging, so don't worry if it takes you a while to learn. Try to connect the notes without letting them ring over each other. You'll hear what I mean when you listen to the recording.

# STUDY IN G MINOR
## (TWO DOWN, ONE UP)

*Jim Kelly*

CLASSICAL STYLE (♩. = 112)

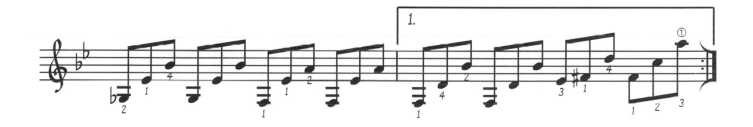

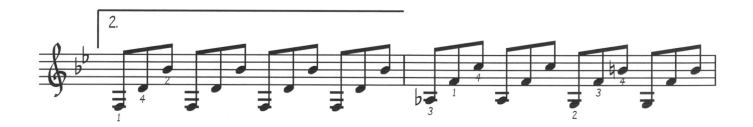

(blank page to facilitate page turn)

# FELLINI

**Audio CD Track**

Solo guitar    6

This is another study for solo guitar. Like "Study in G Minor," it also contains many arpeggios. Here the notes often descend and then ascend through the chords within a one-octave range. The key is D minor, and most measures are played four times. The scale runs are related to A7♭9 and consist of a combination of scales that work on the A7♭9 sound.

This is a technical study. At fast tempos it becomes difficult to pick all the notes of an arpeggio, and even if you can, it may not be the desired sound. When listening to jazz saxophone and piano solos, you will hear these types of quick lines played, but not often as relentlessly as in this study.

The type of picking used here is often called sweep-picking. It is common in rock and metal guitar, usually spanning two or more octaves. You pick down when going from low to high strings and pick up when going from high to low. When two notes fall on the same string, the first is picked and the second is generally played with a hammer or pull-off, depending on the direction of the line.

Most of this study has a pull-off between the first and second notes and a hammer-on between the fifth and sixth notes of each measure. This keeps a consistent legato feel to the piece.

Each arpeggio is really a separate exercise, so you can isolate each section to be worked out. I grew up playing rock and blues in the pre-metal era and, as a result, don't have much experience with this type of picking. I find it to be extremely difficult to play through the whole thing. The goal—in my opinion—is to be able to use these sounds in short, quick spurts. The torture of this exercise should help get these sounds under your fingertips.

The title is a dedication to the late director of Italian cinema, Federico Fellini. I am a fan of his movies and also the music in them. Often the music was written by Nino Rota, one of the all-time great film composers. The chord change between the 4th and 5th bars of the piece put in mind something he would have written for strings.

# Fellini

Jim Kelly

# Meterman

**Audio CD Tracks**
Band          7
Play-along    19 (no guitar)

"Meterman" was written in the style of the New Orleans funk/r&b group called the Meters. The group started in the 70s and has been very influential; a lot of different bands have picked up on this particular groove. It has roots in march music from New Orleans. Some other guys very important to this feel are Professor Longhair, Dr. John, and James Booker. Jazz players such as John Scofield and saxophonist Bennie Wallace sometimes show these influences in their writing.

The Meters' music is mostly instrumental, and is much more about groove than solos. The melody in this tune is a combination of a pentatonic line and some triad rhythm hits. After the melody, the solos are all played over a C7 chord.

On the recording, I stick close to the blues sound. Live, it will often drift more "out," and it can get quite free over the C bass pedal. One important thing to do in these one-chord solo sections is to play phrases. Bob Tamagni does a great job on drums with this groove and plays 4-bar phrases throughout the solo.

The intro is a three-note C7 chord with no 3rd. I like the sound you get by sliding into the ♭7th and the 5th while sustaining the root. Many of the voicings are organ-like. As a matter of fact, the Meters have an organ, so you could add one on this tune if you've got a friend who plays one.

Often when there are chord voicings in this song, I'll strum between the chord hits, keeping a constant rhythm while muting on the rests with the left hand. Basically it is the same approach as in the intro.

This is a good one to learn at a jam session because there is enough form to start things off. Even if it appears simple, try to develop the solo section.

# Meterman

Jim Kelly

FORM: INTRO (16 BARS) HEAD, INTERLUDE, HEAD. SOLOS ON C7. AFTER SOLOS INTERLUDE, HEAD, HEAD (OMIT INTERLUDE).

# MUTT & JEFF

**Audio CD Tracks**

Band            8

Play-along     20 (no guitar on solos)

Intro: 8 bars

In Head: twice

Sax Solo: 3 choruses

Guitar Solo: 4 choruses

Vamp: 4 bars

Out Head: twice

Tag: 8 bars until ending

This jazz-rock-fusion tune was written for a series of gigs in Spain with a Berklee MIDI group. The band consisted of electronic drums, synth keyboard, synth woodwind controller, bass on guitar synth, alto sax, and electric guitar.

The intro was written to be played by a sequencer. Later, I found out we weren't using a sequencer, so the intro turned into a guitar part. The intro is difficult to play, but it's a good picking exercise. It's best in the 5th position using alternate picking. The notes are very staccato (short in length). The syncopation of the notes makes it feel like it's not in 4/4 time, but it is.

The melody and groove of this one are manic and are guaranteed to make you sweat. Playing the shape of the melody is more important than the actual notes. That is, go for the feel and the rhythms, and if an occasional note gets moved, don't panic. At this tempo, many of the lines don't sound like notes anyway.

The solo form consists of 8 bars of G7, 4 bars of E7, and 8 bars of C7. This makes a 20-bar length which is not typical, but makes sense once you hear it a few times.

In the melody, there are many places where I uses slides, hammers, and pull-offs. Check out the articulations on pages 52 and 53, but feel free to change some of them if you find ways that work better for you. Don't worry if some sections are tough; this struggle is part of the sound.

After the solos, the band drops out and the guitar plays 4 bars of the intro. The melody is played twice at the end, like the beginning. For the very end, tag the C7 section ending on the hits in the 6th bar. When you hear the recording it will all make sense.

The recording was done first take, live in the studio. We decided after that it would be too strange to remove the guitar completely, so we reduced the level on the heads, took out the comping behind the sax solo, and removed the guitar solo. Practice the head with the recording and get some friends together to "rip it up" with you.

# Mutt & Jeff

Jim Kelly

Fast Jazz/Rock (♩ = 152)

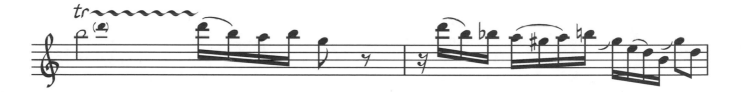

*FORM: Intro (8 bars) head (2 times), solos on form. After solos intro (4 bars), head (2 times), tag last 8 bars until FINE.*

# USED BLUES

**Audio CD Tracks**

Band            10

Play-along      11 (no guitar)

This is a 12-bar blues in the key of C with what I would call a jazz-organ groove. It has a swing feel, and the chord voicings in the melody are the same as an organ player would use. Over the C7, you'll find an Am and a Gm triad: in this case, both with the root in the melody. These triads are typical as harmony in blues and the like. Both triads contain notes that are chord tones and tensions of C9 and C13. One way to find these sounds is to remember that you can use a minor triad built from the 5th and 6th degrees of the 7th chord. The 5th and 6th of the C7 are the notes G and A, so use Gm and Am. This idea is transposed in bar 5 over the F9 chord. Now the two triads are Dm and Cm, from the 6th and 5th of F7. In the 9th bar, the same sound happens over the D9: try to figure out the triad names.

On the third beat of bar 8 you'll find a Bbm triad over the A7 sound. This is more from the jazz school and gives the b9, b13, and 3rd of the A7. It is built on a half-step above the 7th chord. On the 1st beat of the 10th measure, you'll see this sound transposed. Over the G7 you see the Abm triad. In this same measure on beat 2, you'll find a Bbm triad over the G7; this gives #9, b7, and b5 of the G7. These notes are often referred to as altered tensions.

Well, if all this gives you a headache, join the club. Like many things, the theory takes a while to grasp. It will help you to use these sounds in other places. The main thing is to learn what it sounds like, and the rest will follow.

The only chord voicing we didn't discuss is in the last bar. This G7b13 chord voicing is sometimes labeled G7#5, G7+, and Gaug7. All imply the same chord voicing that is used often in jazz.

The recorded version is only the head twice and out—no solos. You can get the feel from listening and then try it with a band. If you add a horn player to the melody, have him play the bottom notes of the chords. For example, the line in the 1st measure would be C, Bb, G, A, C for melody notes. Let's play some blues.

# Used Blues

Jim Kelly

Medium Shuffle Blues (♩ = 120)

(blank page to facilitate page turn)

# Song for an Imaginary Vocal

## (Acoustic Style)

Here is an accompaniment part that is written in a very active style. It consists mainly of eighth notes, and I consider it to be difficult to play. As the title suggests, it sounds like a backing part for a vocal tune. At this point, there is neither a melody nor a vocal part.

One of the hardest things about this study is the picking. Besides alternate picking, many other combinations are available, and often a better choice. I wrote the piece first and then worked on playing it, so the picking gradually evolved. On pages 55–57, you will find some picking suggestions, but I strongly recommend that you try other combinations to find what works best for you.

This is also an endurance exercise since it is played twice with no break. Keeping a steady pulse is tough at first, but when you have played it enough to keep it steady, you'll find it will improve the time feel in other songs where there are a lot of arpeggiated chords. It can be very difficult to play this style behind a vocalist, especially without drums. It's challenging playing on stage in front of a lot of people with just a guitar and vocal. Working on this study can prepare you for playing in this setting.

Listen for the shape of the line. You will notice that dynamics are an important consideration. Also work on making the pull-offs in tempo with the picked notes; it is often uneven when you start.

I think the best thing to do is to play the piece, and things will get clearer as you learn it. Also, try soloing over it and work on pacing since it's such a long form.

# SONG FOR AN IMAGINARY VOCAL
## (ACOUSTIC STYLE)

Jim Kelly

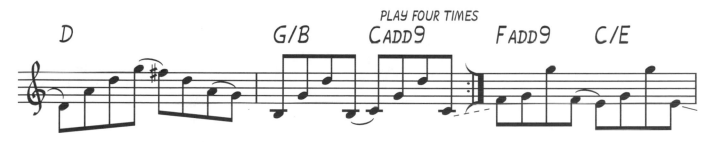

# LATIN-STYLE BLUES

**Audio CD Tracks**

Solo Guitar   14 (pick)

Variation     15 (fingers)

This is a rhythm part that contains only three chord fingerings. Once you get the first 2 bars down, you just have to move it around to the right roots. The first voicing (F13) is followed by a four-note chord stacked in perfect 4ths, a four-note "4th voicing." These voicings can have many names depending on what you are considering to be the root. The second chord is an F7sus4 since F is the root. It would also be correct to call it a Cm11 if you want the bass player to play the note C on the bottom. The third and last voicing is another inversion of an F13. This particular voicing has the root in the melody (on top, as it is often called).

This type of chord voicing (without the root in the bass) is very typical of jazz piano as well as guitar. At first, these chords are hard to hear and use. This progression will help you to plug these chords in and hear how they work. The finger-style variation has the same chords; only the picking is different.

I suggest that you make a tape of yourself playing the chords and practice soloing over it. Try using the F Mixolydian scale over the F7 section, B♭ Mixolydian over the B♭7, and C Mixolydian over the C7. If this is new territory, Mixolydian comprises the 1, 2, 3, 4, 5, 6, and ♭7, and is often used in this style of Latin blues.

# Latin-Style Blues

Jim Kelly

Latin (♩ = 84)

# TABLATURE AND FINGERINGS

In this section, you will find several different styles of guitar-specific notation. Tablature is included as a guide to those who find it helpful, not as an alternative to reading standard music notation. In my estimation, guitar is the hardest instrument to read on, largely because of all the alternate note positions and fingering choices. Many choices are determined by the style and the tempo of the music, and it is often up to the player to find something that works. Surrounding the written music you will find numbers in circles as string references, ① being the high E. Fingers are numbered without circles, and Roman numerals indicate position, adding up to what most likely looks like too much information.

In a one-on-one situation, I prefer to hand out music with few indications and discuss the possibilities. The indications in this section are basically how I am fingering and positioning things, something I still experiment with. These are meant as guidelines. Feel free to change some if you like, just make sure it will work. In many cases, there are choices that work as well and possibly better, but be sure the alternative is solid. This kind of research is an important part of development and will help your playing and reading.

I suggest that when you play with the CD or a group, use the lead sheets at the front of the book. They are similiar to parts usually used in a gigging situation.

# A Little Wes

Medium Up Swing (♩ = 132)

Jim Kelly

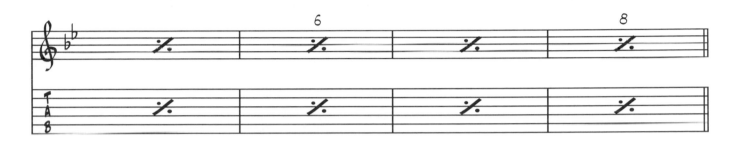

CODA FOR ENDING

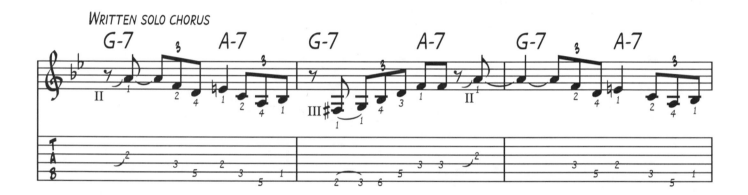

WRITTEN SOLO CHORUS

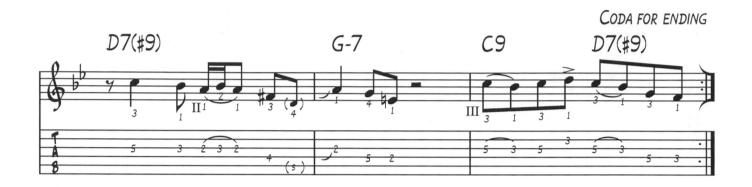

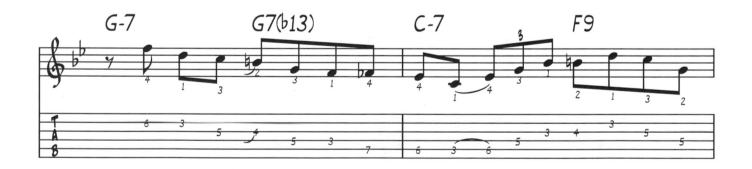

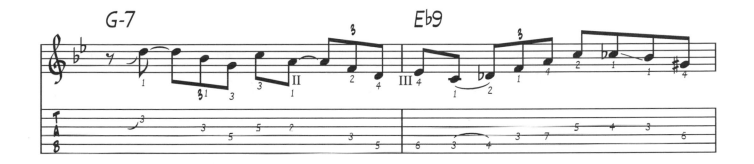

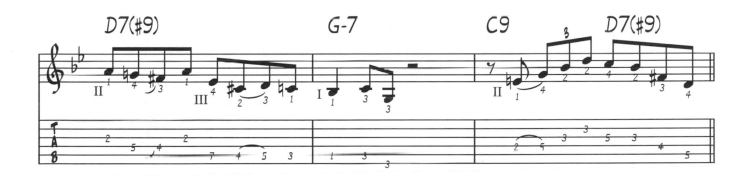

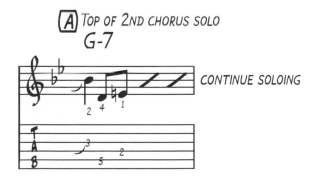

**A** TOP OF 2ND CHORUS SOLO

CONTINUE SOLOING

**⊕** CODA

G-7   A-7

REPEAT & FADE

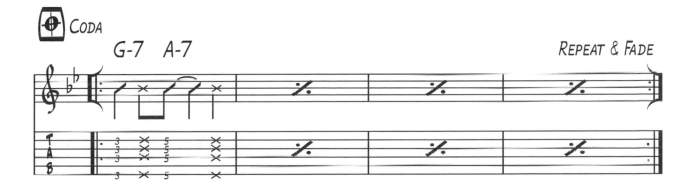

# STILL PRETENDIN'

Jim Kelly

Acoustic 16th Feel (♩ = 88)

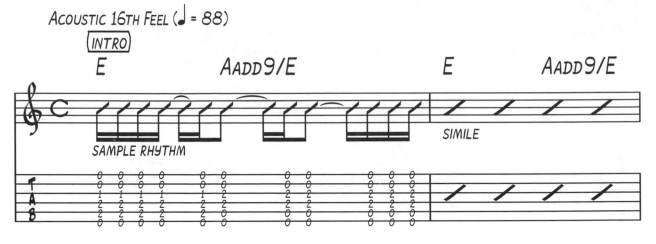

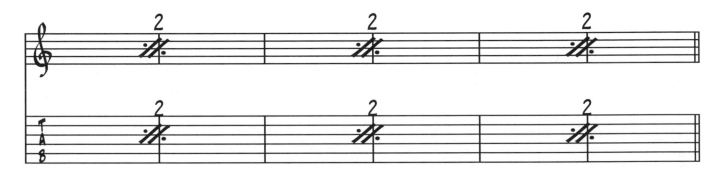

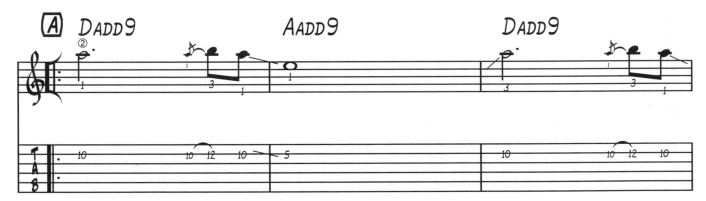

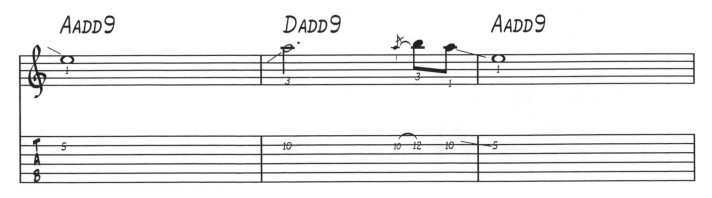

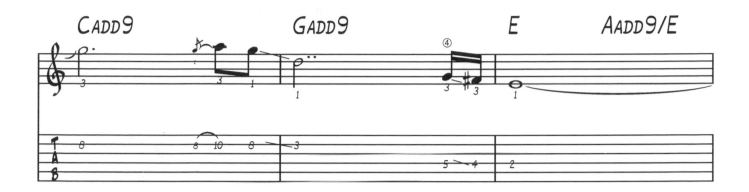

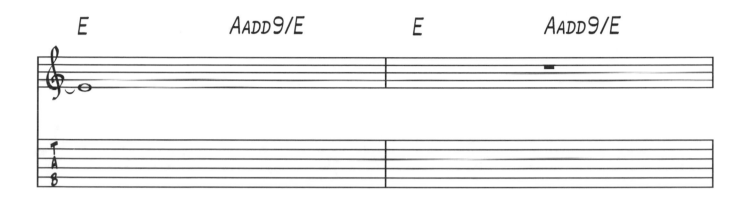

# BOUNCIN' WITH RICK

Jim Kelly

Medium Up Swing ($\quad$ = 126)

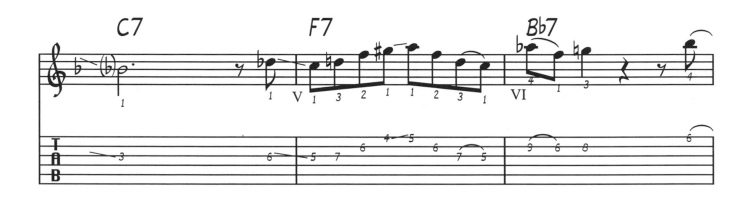

\* Four-bar bass and drum intro on CD only.

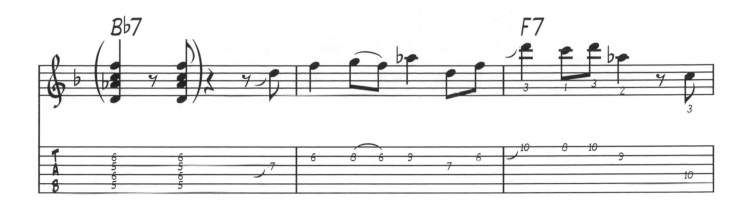

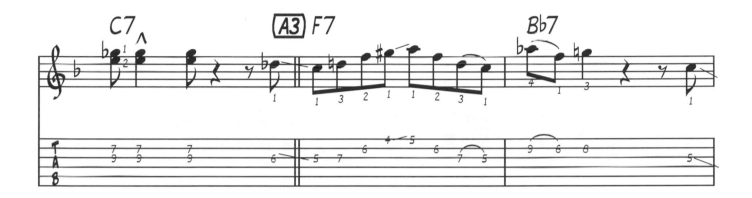

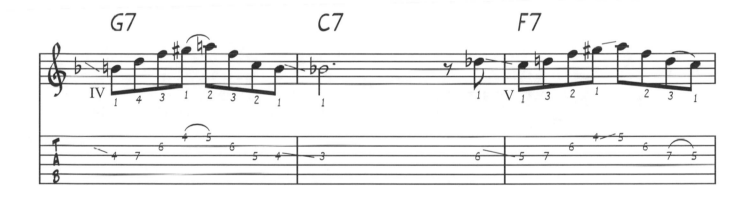

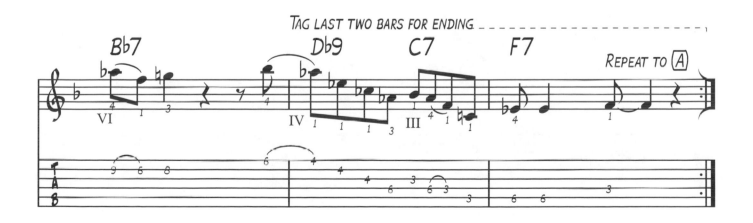

# STUDY IN G MINOR
## (TWO DOWN, ONE UP)

Jim Kelly

CLASSICAL STYLE (♩. = 112)

LET RING THROUGHOUT

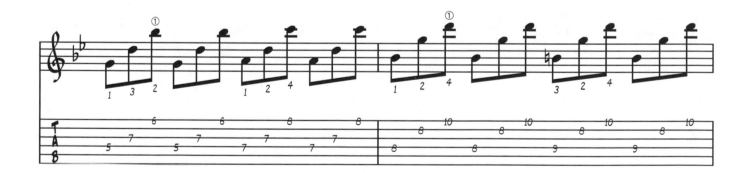

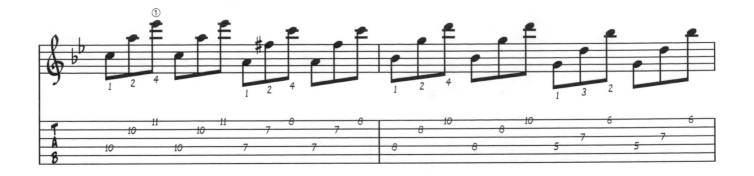

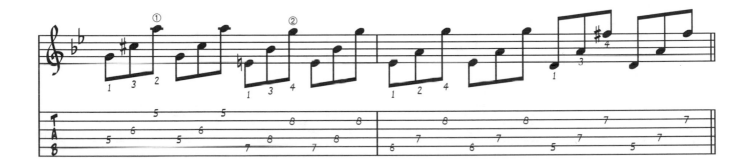

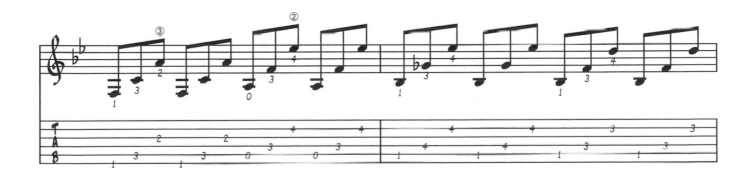

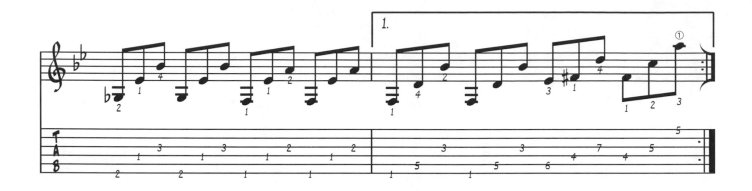

# Fellini

Jim Kelly

Classical Style (♩ = 138)

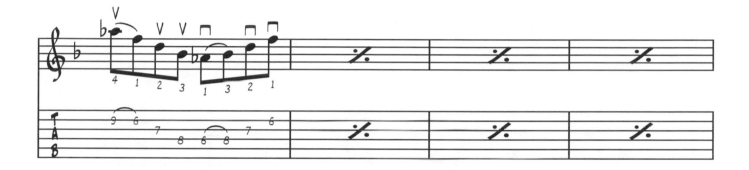

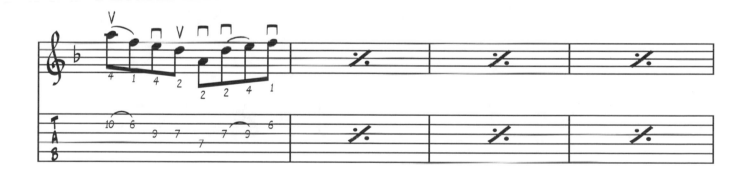

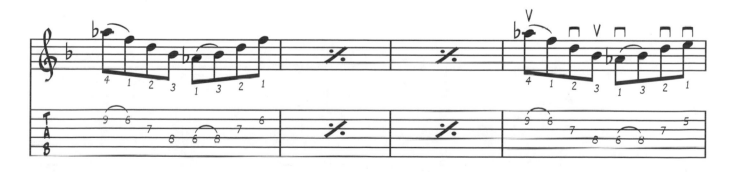

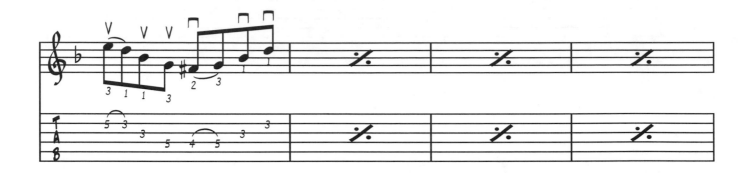

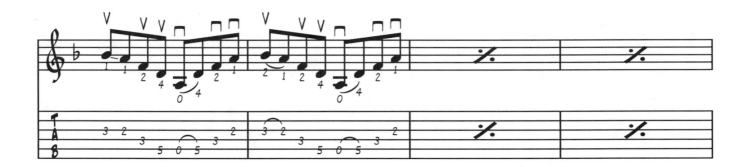

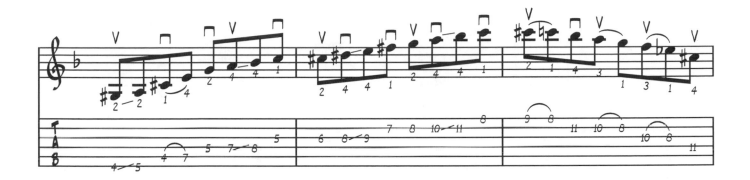

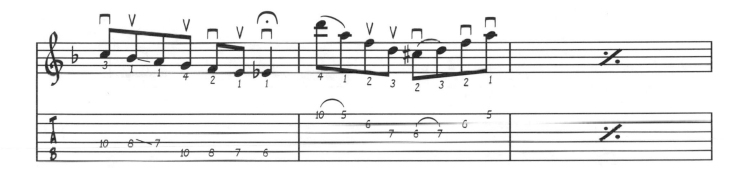

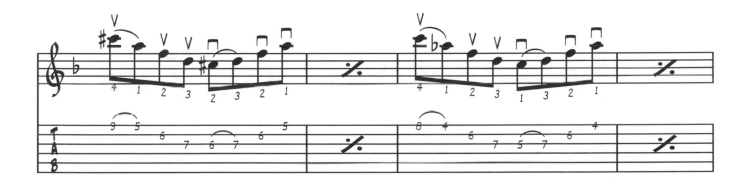

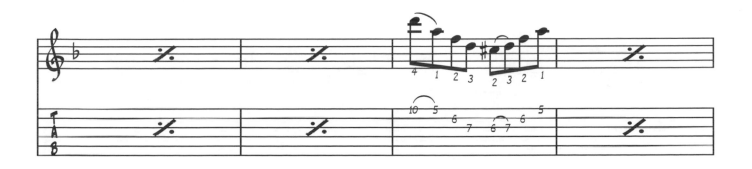

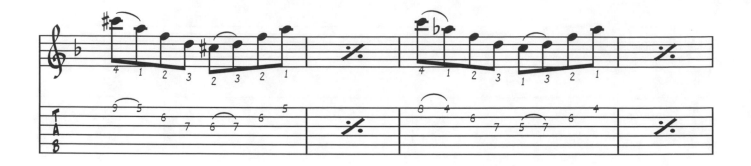

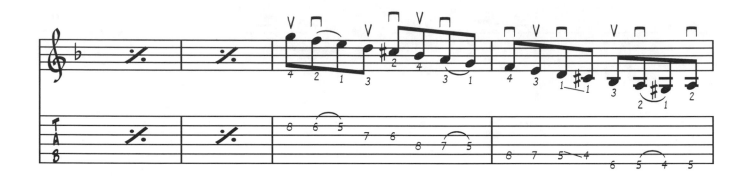

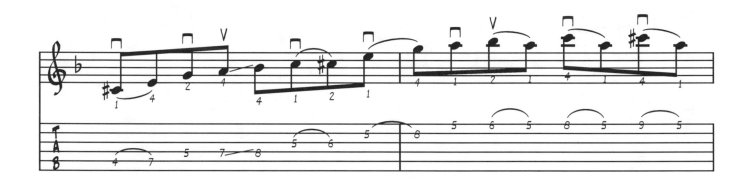

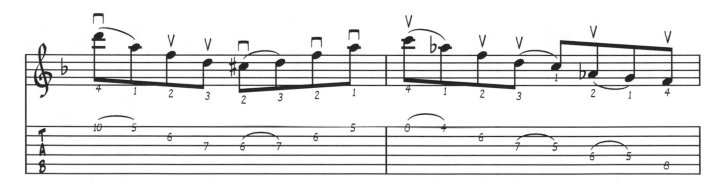

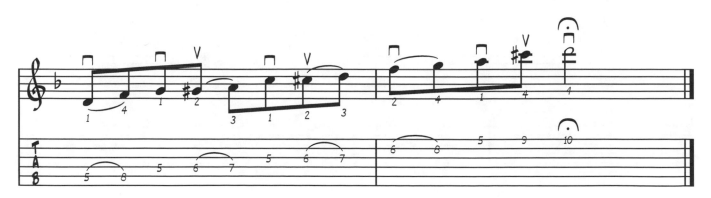

(blank page to facilitate page turn)

# Meterman

Jim Kelly

New Orleans-Style Funk (♩ = 88)

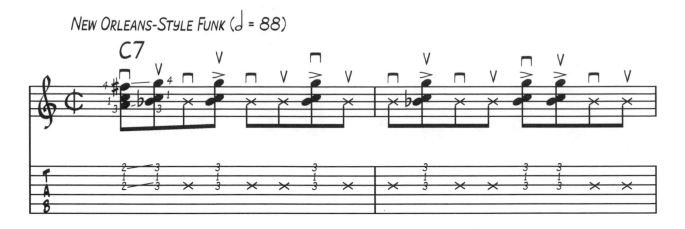

(CONTINUE GROOVE WITH VARIATIONS)

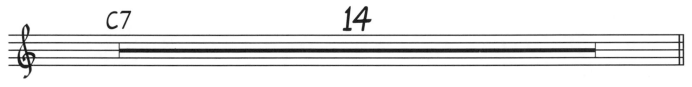

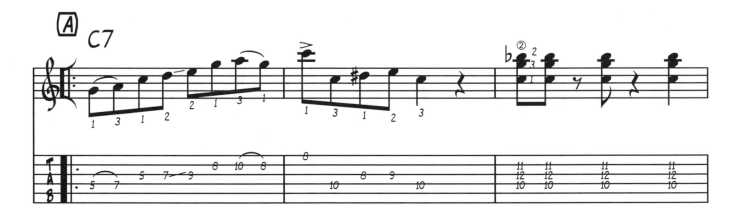

FORM: Intro (16 bars) head, interlude, head. Solos on C7. After solos interlude, head, head (omit interlude).

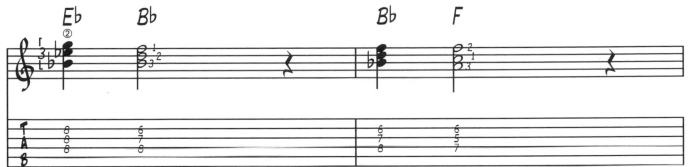

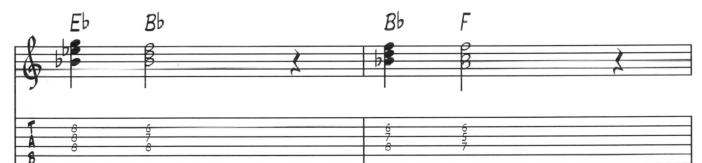

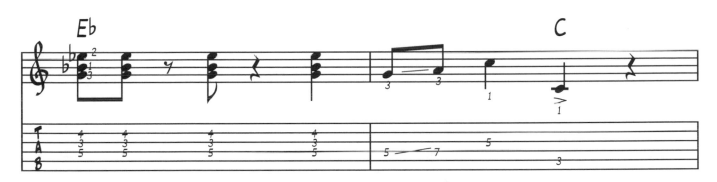

TAG LAST TWO BARS FOR ENDING - - - - - - - - - - - - - - - - - - - - - - -

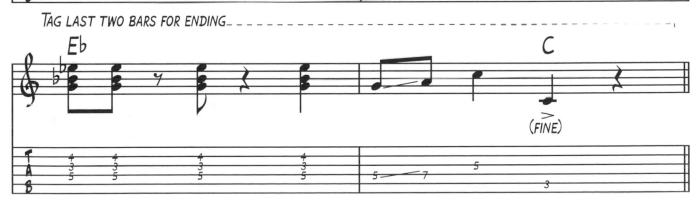

(FINE)

INTERLUDE (LIKE INTRO)
SOLO ON C7 (4-BAR VAMP)

C7                              8

# Mutt & Jeff

Jim Kelly

Fast Jazz/Rock (♩ = 152)

INTRO

FORM: Intro (8 bars) head (2 times), solos on form. After solos intro (4 bars), head (2 times), tag last 8 bars until FINE.

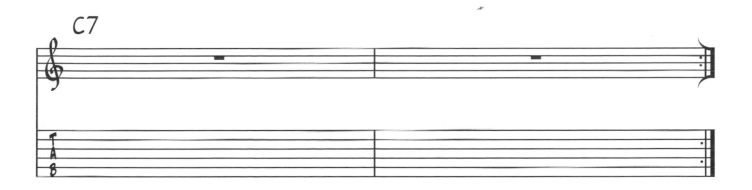

# USED BLUES

JIM KELLY

MEDIUM SHUFFLE BLUES (♩ = 120)

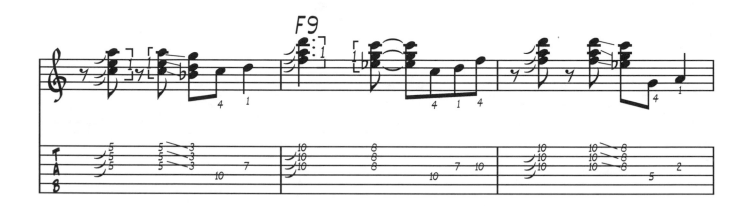

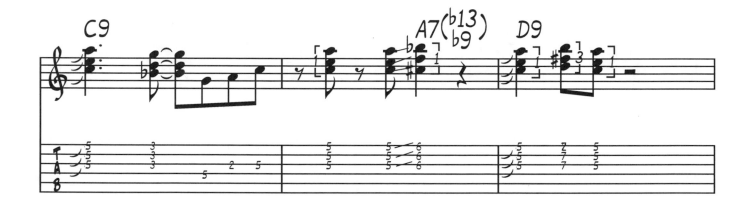

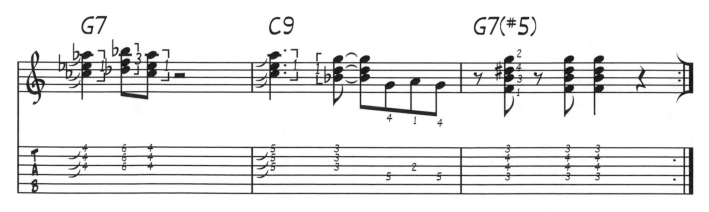

# Song for an Imaginary Vocal
### (Acoustic Style)

Jim Kelly

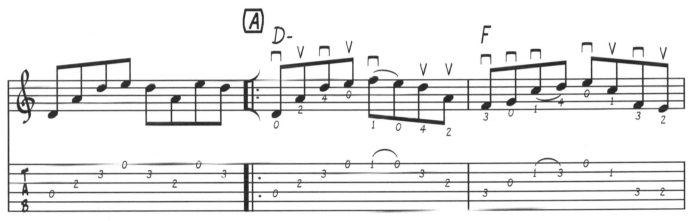

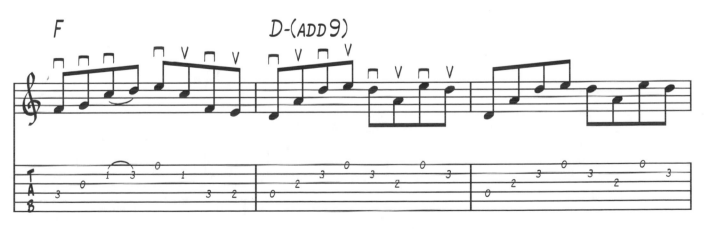

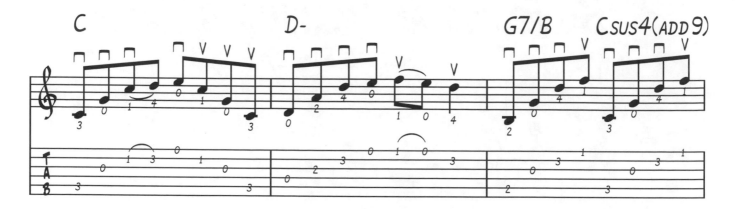

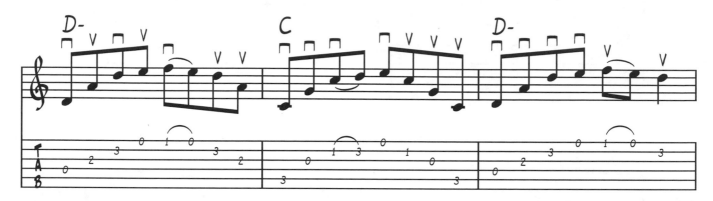

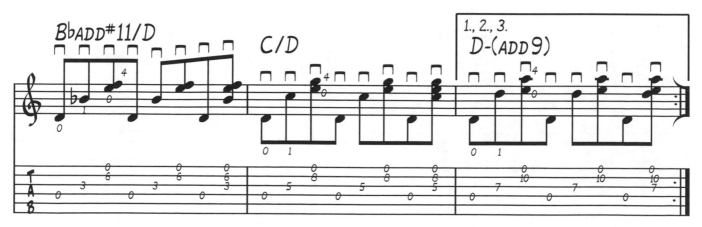

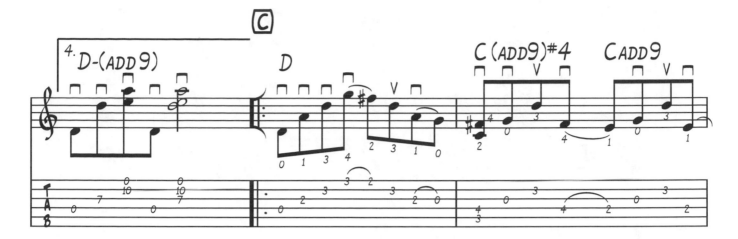

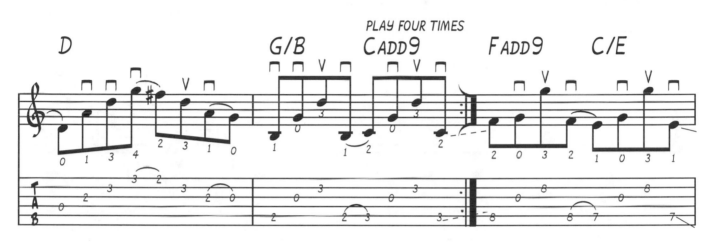

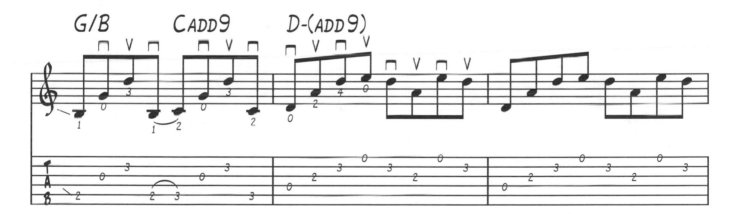

NOTE: THE D-(ADD 9) VOICING USED IN THIS PIECE OMITS THE MINOR THIRD.

AN ALTERNATE PICKING CHOICE FOR MEASURE 1 IS ⊓ ⊓ ⊓ ⊓  V V ⊓ V.

# LATIN-STYLE BLUES

Jim Kelly

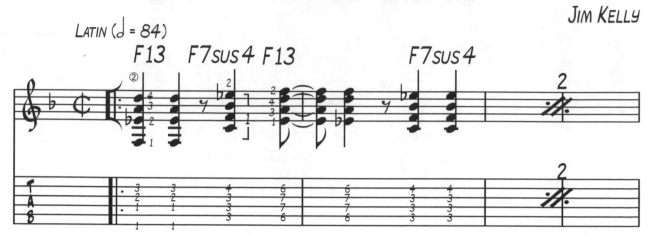

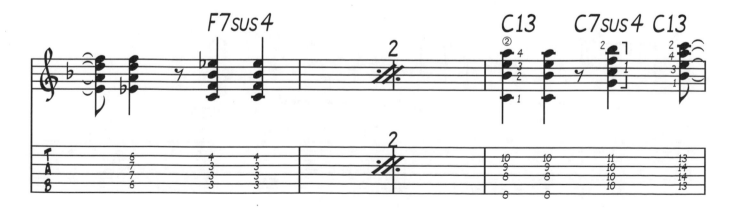

## LATIN-STYLE BLUES (FINGER VARIATION)

NOTE: FINGERING WILL BE THE SAME FOR LATIN-STYLE BLUES VARIATION.

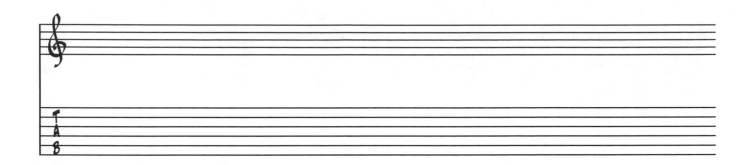

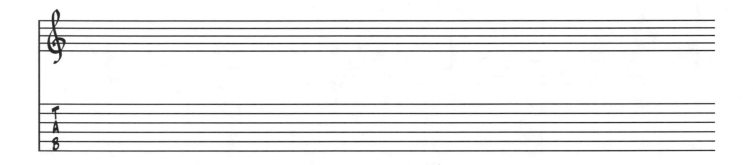

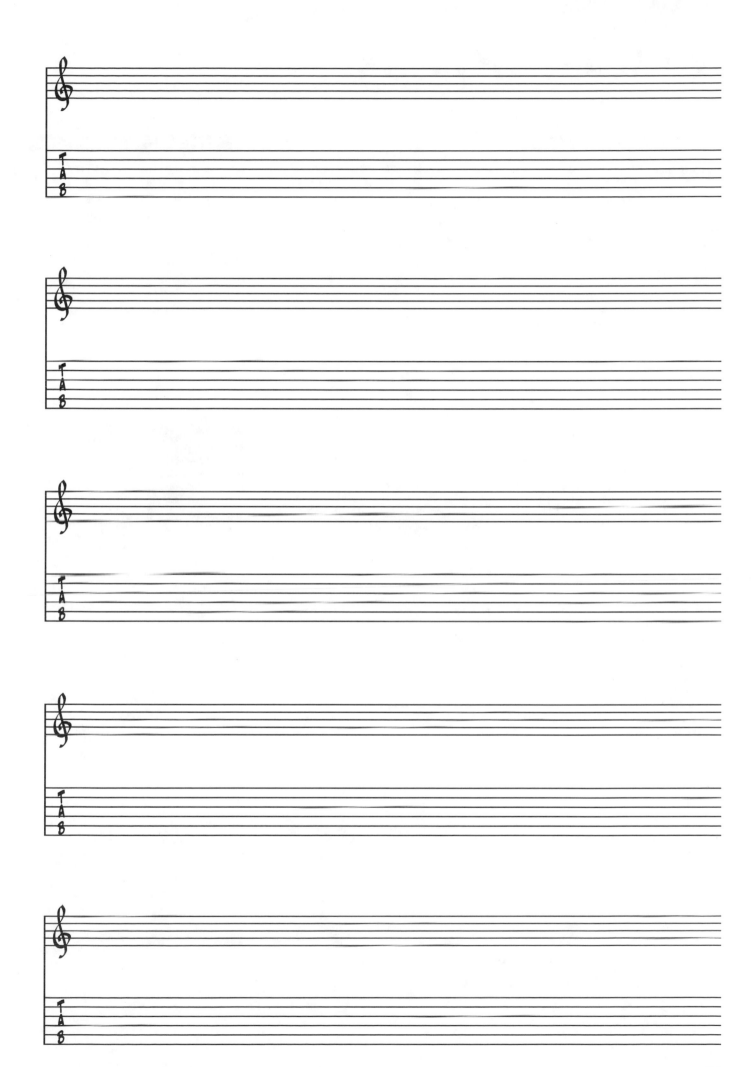

# Berklee Press

*These books feature material used at the famous Berklee College of Music.*

## GENERAL INSTRUCTION

### A MODERN METHOD FOR GUITAR
*by William Leavitt*

A practical and comprehensive guitar method in three volumes, designed for the serious student and used as the basic text for the Berklee College of Music guitar program. With this unique approach, the student develops technique in both hands as he/she learns to read music. Innovative solos, duets, and exercises progressively teach melody, harmony, and rhythm. For beginning through advanced levels of playing, this is the method that has inspired tremendous loyalty among teachers and students. Demonstration audio is now available for the first two volumes, either sold separately or as a book/tape package.

### VOLUME 1

A beginning level book presenting a comprehensive range of guitar and music fundamentals. Included are scales, melodic studies, chord and arpeggio studies, special exercises for both hands, accompaniment techniques, and a unique approach to voice leading using movable chord forms.

_____50449400  Book ................................$12.95
_____50449404  Book/CD Pack **NEW!** ........$22.95
_____50449402  Book/Cassette Pack...........$18.95
_____50449401  Cassette Only.......................$7.95

### VOLUME 2

Continues the study of melody, scales, arpeggios, and chords, covering the entire fingerboard. Written at the intermediate level, this volume addresses intervals, chord voicings, and improvisation, and includes special sections on rhythm guitar techniques. The cassette features "play-along" duets; each duet part is recorded separately so that the student can play along.

_____50449410  Book ................................$12.95
_____50449412  Book/Cassette Pack...........$18.95
_____50449411  Cassette Only.......................$7.95

### VOLUME 3

A continuation and expansion of topics presented in volumes 1 and 2. Includes advanced techniques relating to scales, arpeggios, rhythm guitar, chord-scale relationships, chord construction, and chord voicings. Also includes playing tips.

_____50449420  Book ................................$12.95

### THE GUITAR, PHASE I
*by William Leavitt*

An ideal method for the beginning guitar student or guitar class. Technique and reading skills are developed through two-, three-, and four-part ensemble arrangements of traditional and newly composed music. An introduction to chords is also included. A cassette demonstrates the ideal performance.

_____50449460  Book (B-29-1)....................$7.95
_____50449462  Book/Cassette Pack...........$14.95

### THE GUITAR, PHASE II
*by William Leavitt*

A continuation of Phase I, this phase includes solo, two-part, and three-part ensemble arrangements of traditional and newly composed music for the beginning to intermediate student or class. Skills are developed through delightful arrangements of music by Bach, Foster, Leavitt, Schumann, and others.

_____50449470  (B-29-2) ............................$7.95

### ADVANCED READING STUDIES FOR GUITAR
*by William Leavitt*

For the guitarist who wants to improve reading ability in positions 8 through 12, 112 pages of progressive studies written especially for the guitar, in all keys, and consisting of scales, arpeggios, intervals, and notated chords in various time signatures. A special section of multi-position studies is included. An important method for all guitarists who want to learn the entire fingerboard.

_____50449500  (B-60) ..............................$10.95

### READING CONTEMPORARY RHYTHMS
*by M.T. Szymczak*

A collection of 52 harmonized melodies and 31 rhythm exercises designed to increase reading skills. Sixteenth note patterns are emphasized. Notated chords and rhythm guitar accompaniments provide excellent solos and duets.

_____50449530............................................$10.95

### READING STUDIES FOR GUITAR
*by William Leavitt*

A comprehensive collection of studies for improving reading and technical ability. Includes scales, arpeggios, written-out chords, and a variety of rhythms and time signatures. Positions 1 through 7 are covered in all keys. An important method for all guitarists who recognize the advantages of being able to sight-read.

_____50449490............................................$10.95

## STYLISTIC INSTRUCTION

### COUNTRY GUITAR STYLES
*by Mike Ihde*

For the guitarist who wants to learn the secrets of playing "country." Complete with detailed explanations, illustrations, notated examples, full-length solos, and a demonstration cassette tape. Styles and effects include country rhythm, single-note lead, pedal steel, bluegrass, finger-picking, western, rockabilly, Memphis style, harmonics, string bending, electronic effects, and more.

_____50449480  Book/Cassette Pack...........$14.95

### ROCK GUITAR STYLES
*by Mike Ihde*

This popular hands-on book will teach the modern guitarist how to play lead and rhythm guitar. Styles include heavy metal, hard rock, new wave, blues, jazz-rock, funk, and more. Electronic equipment is also discussed. Five additional arrangements for lead guitar, rhythm guitar, bass, and drums are included. Many music examples and a demonstration cassette make this the player's method of choice. Includes a 33-minute audio accompaniment.

_____50449520  Book/Cassette Pack...........$14.95

### MELODIC RHYTHMS FOR GUITAR
*by William Leavitt*

A thorough presentation of rhythms commonly found in contemporary music, including 68 harmonized melodies and 42 rhythm exercises. This is also an excellent source for duets, sight-reading, and chord studies. The cassette features demonstration duets as well as recorded rhythm section accompaniments so that the student can play melodies along with the tape.

_____50449450  Book ................................$10.95
_____50449452  Book/Cassette Pack...........$16.95

### CLASSICAL STUDIES FOR PICK-STYLE GUITAR
*by William Leavitt*

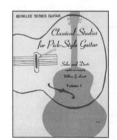

An outstanding collection of solos and duets for intermediate to advanced pick-style guitarists. Includes 21 pieces by Carcassi, Carulli, Sor, Bach, Paganini, Kreutzer and Clementi.

_____50449440............................................$8.95

### GUITAR DUETS – VOLUME 1
*by William Leavitt*

A collection of seven duets composed and arranged by William Leavitt. Chords and melody are skillfully blended, resulting in challenging and enjoyable music for intermediate and advanced guitarists. Guitar parts are separately bound.

_____50449430  (B-37-1) ..............................$7.95

### CHORD STUDIES FOR ELECTRIC BASS
*by Rich Appleman/Joseph Viola*

This 162-page method thoroughly covers basic and extended chords in all keys. Melodic studies designed for the intermediate and advanced player develop all aspects of technique. Special emphasis is placed on playing in the higher register. This method can also be effectively used for acoustic bass study.

_____50449750...........................................$12.95

### READING CONTEMPORARY ELECTRIC BASS RHYTHMS
*by Rich Appleman*

A comprehensive collection of exercises and performance studies designed to enable the student to play in a wide range of musical styles. Includes funk, rock, disco, jazz, top 40, soft rock, and country western. Excellent for sight-reading and technical development.

_____50449770...........................................$10.95

### MUSIC NOTATION
*by Mark McGrain*

A practical and straightforward text for anyone who needs to notate music properly. It's as useful to the first year theory student as it is to professional arrangers and composers. Helpful exercises, common practice rules, and simple language make this a valuable reference guide for all musicians.

_____50449399  207 Pages..........................$16.95

### MANAGING LYRIC STRUCTURE
*by Pat Pattison*

This book will help songwriters handle lyric structures more effectively. If you have written lyrics before, this book will help you gain even greater control and understanding of your craft. If you have not written lyrics before, this book will get you off in a healthy direction. You will find information in this book about lyric structure and exercises to help you make it part of your own writing. This book will show you ways to say things better. It will help you manage timing and placement. That is the point of structure. By the time you finish, not only will you be a better writer, but you will know more about lyric structure than you ever thought possible.

_____50481582...........................................$11.95

### RHYMING TECHNIQUES AND STRATEGIES
*by Pat Pattison*

This book has been designed to help you find better rhymes and use them more effectively. If you have written lyrics before, maybe even professionally, and you want to take a new look or gain even greater control and understanding of your craft, this book could be just the thing for you. If you have never written lyrics before, this book will help. You won't have a chance to develop bad habits.

_____50481583...........................................$10.95

Jim Kelly's Guitar Workshop products are an integrated, interactive, instructional approach to helping guitarists improve their playing through songs and studies in jazz, blues, Latin, R&B, and more. The songs that Jim Kelly has written for this series are designed to help you learn how to play in the style of guitar greats like Jeff Beck, Kenny Burrell, Mike Stern, Pat Metheny, Wes Montgomery, Joe Pass, Stevie Ray Vaughan, and others. Listen to Jim capture the sound of these players, and then use the play-along tracks to develop your own approaches. The tunes in this series represent a cross-section of modern guitar styles and song forms.

With full-band and play-along tracks, you will learn how to phrase your own solos in new ways by using the techniques of master guitar players. Jim Kelly presents these ideas clearly throughout the books, audio CDs, video tapes, and DVD products in this series.

Valuable to players at all levels, the strong melodies and chord changes are fun to listen to and learn. Jim and his band knock-out each tune so you can hear how it sounds featuring quartet and trio tracks with alto sax, acoustic and electric guitars, bass, and drums. The books provide you with traditional lead sheet music notation and guitar tablature, including style, tempo, form, fingerings, song description and commentary, hints, tips, approach and practice ideas.

### JIM KELLY'S GUITAR WORKSHOP BOOK/CD PACK
_____00695230  Book/CD Pack...................$14.95

### MORE JIM KELLY'S GUITAR WORKSHOP BOOK/CD PACK
_____00695306  Book/CD Pack...................$14.95

### JIM KELLY'S GUITAR WORKSHOP VIDEO
_____00320144  Video/Booklet ..................$19.95

### MORE JIM KELLY'S GUITAR WORKSHOP VIDEO
_____00320158  Video/Booklet ..................$19.95

### COMING SOON:
• JIM KELLY'S GUITAR WORKSHOP SERIES DVD

## About the Author

Jim Kelly is a professor of Guitar at Berklee College of Music. One of the cornerstones of the guitar faculty, Kelly has traveled the world, teaching and performing throughout Europe, South America, and Japan in the college's "On the Road" series of clinics. For over 20 years, Jim has worked closely with several thousand aspiring guitarists, building their technique, feel, and confidence. For many years, he has been one of the most requested guitar teachers on the faculty.

Kelly plays in a variety of settings that helps give a diverse but practical edge to his teaching. He has performed with swing blues guitarist Duke Robillard, the contemporary musical *Rent*, rock singer Peter Wolf, and many great Berklee alumni including Makoto Ozone, Stu Hamm, Bill Frisell, Gary Chaffee, John Abercrombie, and Gary Burton. The band on the CD is his group the Sled Dogs, which has long been an outlet for his compositions and guitar playing. They have a release on RAM Records titled "The Music of Jim Kelly."

## About Berklee Press

Berklee Press is the official publishing arm of the world-renowned Berklee College of Music, a premier institution for music study. Berklee Press publishes high-quality practical books, videotapes, DVDs, and interactive products for all areas of contemporary music education including performance, ear training, harmony, composition, songwriting, arranging, film scoring, music therapy, production, engineering, music business, synthesis, and music technology. Berklee Press products are dedicated to furthering the enrichment and success of musicians, students, teachers, and hobbyists alike.

## Berklee College of Music

Founded in Boston in 1945, Berklee College of Music is the world's largest independent music college and the premier institution for the study of contemporary music. The college's 3,000 students and 300 faculty members interact in an environment that includes all of the opportunities presented by a career in the contemporary music industry. Our faculty and alumni are among the finest musicians in the world.

For more information about Berklee Press or Berklee College of Music, contact us:

Berklee Press
1140 Boylston Street
Boston, MA  02215-3693
berkleepress.com
617-747-2146